D0707643

Real-World math
for Grades 4-6

Connecting Classroom Skills to Students' Everyday Lives

by

Susan R. O'Connell

Dedicated to
Jack and Jenny O'Connell

Senior Editor: Kristin Eclov
Editor: Lisa Trumbauer
Interior Design: Amy Dohmen
Interior Illustration: Emilie Kong
Cover Design: Stephanie Berman

Good Apple
A Division of Frank Schaffer Publications, Inc.
23740 Hawthorne Boulevard
Torrance, CA 90505

ISBN 0-7682-0100-4

Table of Contents

INTRODUCTION 5

FAMILY LETTER 8

REAL-WORLD CONNECTIONS 9

    Newspaper Number Search 11

    The Math Problem 12

    Math All Around Us 13

    Real-World Number Problems 14

    How I Used Math Today 15

DINING OUT 16

    Food-and-Fun Family Restaurant 18

    Video-Game Change 19

    Buddy's Bagels 20

    Buying Bagels 21

    Bagel Possibilities 22

    Bagel Glyph 23

    Home-Style Family Restaurant 24

    Burger Barn Design Contest 25

    Burger Barn Design Grid 26

    Grand Opening Celebration 27

    Burger Barn Problem Solving 28

    How Many Should You Order? 29

IN THE KITCHEN 30

    Sold by the Pound 32

    The Corner Market 33

    Shopping List 34

    Super Snack Mix 35

    Snack Riddles 36

    Create a Snack Mix 37

    Rating Snacks 38

    The Cookie Sheet 40

SPORTS 42

    Baseball Abbreviations 44

    Comparing Baseball Players 45

Table of Contents

How Tall Are They? 46

Through the Years 47

Baseball Glyph 48

Batting Averages Bar Graph 49

Most Valuable Player 50

Baseball Brochure 51

Ballpark Birthday 52

Picnic at the Ballpark 53

Plotting the Hits 54

Bowling Tournament 55

Scoring Baskets 56

Home or Away? 57

TRAVEL AND ENTERTAINMENT 59

Weather Map Travels 61

Family Fun Parks 64

Aquarium Adventure 66

Birthday Plans 67

Souvenir Bags 68

Refreshments 69

Party Decorations 70

Music to Your Ears 71

What Are the Chances? 72

Classroom Games 74

Games List 75

REAL-WORLD LITERATURE CONNECTIONS 76

ANSWER KEY 77

30
30
+ 20
——
80

14 x 4 = 56

$12.00
+ $7.00
————
$19.00

Introduction

Students are often unable to see the connection between the math skills they learn in class and events in their everyday lives. When students are unable to understand the usefulness of the skills they learn, they may not appreciate the need to learn each skill. The National Council of Teachers of Mathematics has recommended that teachers focus on helping students make these connections. Their *Curriculum and Evaluation Standards for School Mathematics* (Reston, Virginia: N.C.T.M., 1989) clearly emphasizes making connections as an important consideration in designing classroom lessons.

Focusing students' attention on the math that appears around them every day is one way to help them make connections. For example, pointing out the use of fractions in recipes, comparing numbers in daily weather forecasts, figuring a baseball player's batting average, or calculating percentages for sales tax and restaurant tips provides students with evidence that math is, indeed, used daily in activities outside the classroom. Giving students opportunities to discover the math around them, then providing them with opportunities to discuss where and when math appears, helps focus their attention on real-world connections.

MAKING CONNECTIONS WITH REAL-WORLD MATERIALS

Incorporating authentic materials into classroom lessons also helps to connect math to students' lives. Newspapers, restaurant menus, baseball cards, travel brochures, and sporting-goods catalogs, for example, naturally illustrate the connection between classroom skills and the application of those skills. Throughout this book, you will see ideas for incorporating authentic materials into math lessons. Materials that students recognize as "real world" and "close to home" motivate and excite them. And the use of these materials provides a more realistic math experience.

THE VALUE OF PERFORMANCE TASKS

A performance task is an activity that requires students to use higher-level thinking and problem-solving skills to perform, produce, or create something. The format of a performance task is open-ended and allows students to approach each problem in a variety of ways. The format offers students an opportunity to communicate mathematical thinking through group work and classroom discussions. Many of the activities in this book are performance tasks. They ask students to solve real-life problems and often ask them to explain their strategies or problem-solving choices, with the justification of "how" and "why" the problem was solved in that manner. In many cases, there is more than one answer, and only students' work and explanations demonstrate whether they have understood and effectively completed the task.

ASSESSING PERFORMANCE TASKS

Allowing students options, such as who will join them on an imaginary trip to the amusement park or what they will choose to eat from a restaurant menu, increases students' involvement and motivation. However, it also leads to the possibility of more than one correct answer. Assessing a student's response requires teachers to look at each individual answer and determine if the student has accurately completed the task. A scoring scale, or rubric, is a helpful assessment tool. With a rubric, teachers can consider several skills necessary to perform a task, and they can assess the degree to which students are able to complete the task. Sample rubrics have been provided for one performance task in each section of this book.

The first step in creating a rubric is to determine the "expected student outcomes" for the task. The teacher can then design a scoring scale based on the level to which the student meets these outcomes. In this book, the rubrics are on a 5-point (0–4) scale. Rubrics may be designed on other point scales depending on the complexity of the task.

When scoring student work with a rubric, it is important to review the rubric with students so they understand their scores and are able to see how their scores might improve. Allowing students the opportunity to redo a task after comparing their initial attempt with the rubric lets them address the items they missed in their first attempt. Students will be able to see how a "2" can become a "3" with some additional information, or a "3" can become a "4" if they explain their thinking. Rubrics allow students to see their growth and allow teachers to assess students' ability to "put it all together."

FITTING REAL-WORLD ACTIVITIES INTO YOUR MATH PROGRAM

Real-world activities should be a frequent part of your math program. It is important for students to repeatedly see real-world applications for the math skills you teach. The activities in this book provide suggestions for obtaining this goal. Activities may be used as a classroom lesson, a home assignment, a warm-up to a skills lesson, an assessment task, or an independent activity at a real-world math center. The use of authentic materials is especially suited to centers. For example, restaurant menus or travel brochures can help students select a meal or plan a trip. The Math Skills Chart, located in the introduction of each section, shows the skills being focused on in each activity.

 ## HOME-SCHOOL CONNECTION

Home involvement is often critical for student success. Throughout this book, many activities are labeled with a home-school connection icon. Use these activities as traditional homework assignments or as joint parent/child projects. In addition, the Family Letter on page 8 outlines some home activities that may help students recognize the many ways math is important in their lives. The more clearly parents see the connection between classroom math and math in the real world, the better able they are to point out those connections to their children. Parents who believe that math is critical for success in life are more likely to raise children who believe the same.

USING CALCULATORS TO SUPPORT PROBLEM SOLVING

There are many activities in this book that require students to perform calculations as part of a problem-solving investigation. It is up to you to determine if calculators should be given to students to help them with these activities. While the knowledge of basic operations is critical for success in mathematics, there are times when an emphasis is placed on developing reasoning and problem-solving skills. At these times, calculators support students by allowing them to focus on the investigation. When authentic materials are used, calculators often allow students to perform tasks that they might otherwise be unable to perform because of the complexity of the real data.

HOW THIS BOOK IS ORGANIZED

This book is divided into five sections—*Real-World Connections, Dining Out, In the Kitchen, Sports,* and *Travel and Entertainment*. Each section has two components—teacher pages and student pages. The teacher pages preface each section. They contain instructions for incorporating the math activities into your lessons and any additional information you might need to make the activity go smoothly. You will also find related literature connections and suggestions for using real-world materials. The teacher pages conclude with an assessment suggestion, choosing one activity and detailing a possible rubric scoring system. The student pages are activity sheets and other reproducibles to help students make real-world math connections.

LINKING REAL-WORLD LITERATURE AND MATH

Stories capture students' interest and set the scene for exploring math. Throughout this book you will find references to children's books that support math learning. You might choose to begin each math lesson with a story. This can provide a context for the math lesson, as well as excite and involve students. Including math-related literature in your classroom library reinforces the connection between math and the real world.

THE VALUE OF REAL-WORLD MATH LESSONS

This book provides a variety of open-ended math investigations that require students to apply their classroom skills and gather real data, often by using authentic materials. In addition, they require students to use their reasoning skills to formulate plans and determine effective strategies for problem solving. By using real-world data and topics that interest students (food, entertainment, travel, sports), these investigations direct their attention to everyday math applications, making the connection that math is important in their lives, both today and in the future.

Family Letter

Dear Family,

Throughout the school year, I will be introducing students to many new math skills and strengthening their understanding of others. Along with understanding and mastering math, it is important that students recognize the importance of math in their lives. I will be introducing lessons that show students how math is used at the baseball field, at birthday parties, in the kitchen, and more. It is my hope that students who recognize math in the "real world" will become more enthusiastic about learning it.

You can help your child make this connection, too. Take time each evening to look over your child's homework. Then talk with him or her about the way you used math that day. Below are some home activities that emphasize the role of math in everyday life:

- Look for examples of math around your home or in your neighborhood, for example, the use of measurement in recipes, prices in newspaper grocery ads, checking weather forecasts, and so on.

- Take your child grocery shopping. Have your child estimate weights in the produce section, help you decide on the least expensive cereal, or estimate the cost of purchases before they are totaled. Or, use grocery ads to plan a shopping trip and calculate how much money will be needed.

- Read the sports section of the newspaper with your child. Help your child understand the statistics for a sport or team he or she enjoys.

- When visiting a restaurant, have your child calculate the cost of the menu items he or she selected. Let your child estimate the total cost of the bill.

- Select a dinner recipe with your child and prepare the meal together. Talk about the math needed for preparation, such as measurements, oven temperatures, cooking times, and so on.

- Plan a trip to the movies with your child. Ask him or her to check the newspaper for times and calculate the cost of admission.

These are just a few examples that help children make the connection between classroom math and real-world math. Encourage your child to see that math is all around us. Together we can help your child understand the importance of developing good math skills.

Thank you for your help!

Yours truly,

© 1998 Good Apple GA1686

Real-World Connections

This section highlights general activities that support the idea of math in the real world. Students are asked to notice the numbers around them and understand how they are used. In this way, students are led to realize that math can and does relate to their daily lives.

MATH SKILLS CHART

Real-World Connections Math Skills Chart	Problem Solving	Reasoning/Logic	Communication	Connections	Numeration	Whole Number Operations	Measurement	Data Analysis	Geometry	Rationals (Fractions/Decimals)	Probability/Statistics	Patterns
Newspaper Number Search	x	x	x	x	x		x	x		x	x	x
The Math Problem	x	x	x	x	x	x	x	x	x	x	x	x
Math All Around Us	x	x	x	x		x	x	x	x	x	x	x
Real-World Number Problems	x	x	x	x	x	x						
How I Used Math Today	x	x	x	x								

USING THE PAGES

Newspaper Number Search (page 11)

Bring in the daily newspaper for students to locate numbers. You might save newspapers over several days, or give different sections to partners or small groups. Challenge students to circle all the numbers they see. You might set a time limit, say five minutes. Have students share the numbers they find with the class. Encourage the class to come up with categories for the numbers, such as dates, measurements, ages, game scores, and so on. Finally, invite students to consider the numbers they found during their newspaper search as they write about numbers on the activity sheet.

The Math Problem (page 12)

Speculate with students instances during the school day that require math. If they did not know math, how could these situations be a problem? Guide students to examples such as dividing the class into teams, buying lunch, keeping to a schedule, helping prepare dinner, and so on. Encourage students to write three math problems.

Math All Around Us (page 13)

Invite students to create a poster to show how math is all around us. Pass out the activity sheets, and review with students the topics, or themes. Have students choose the theme for their posters, then write in which ways they think they will discover that math is used. For the next several days, have students be on the look out for how mathematics are related to their themes. For example, if the theme is baseball, students could find player statistics, game scores, catalogs with baseball equipment that show prices, baseball cards, a baseball schedule, ticket prices to a ballpark, and the dimensions of the baseball diamond. When students have collected enough materials, instruct them to arrange their findings on poster board to share with the class.

Real-World Number Problems (page 14)

Challenge students to figure out the number problems. Point out that the numbers relate to real-world examples. Encourage students to write their own "real-world" number problems, too.

How I Used Math Today (page 15)

This activity may be used for only one day, or over several days. You might also incorporate it into students' writing journals. At the end of the school day, invite students to reflect how they used math. For example, did they watch the clock during the day? Did they count change in the lunch room? Did they divide playing pieces during a group activity? Did they keep score during kickball? Instruct students to describe their daily math experiences.

LITERATURE CONNECTION

Janice VanCleave's Math for Every Kid: Easy Activities That Make Math Learning Fun provides an entertaining look at math concepts through activities and problem solving.

REAL-WORLD MATERIALS

One of the best and most easily accessible real-world resources is the daily newspaper. It offers clear evidence that math is part of all areas of life. Many newspapers offer special rates for classroom teachers who would like to purchase sets for classroom use. Contact your local newspaper to learn about any special school programs they offer.

ASSESSMENT SUGGESTION

Task: *Math All Around Us*

Expected Student Outcomes

- creates a real-world math poster that depicts a variety of math examples related to a theme
- creates a title for the poster and labels objects on the poster

Scoring Rubric

4—creates a poster with a variety of math examples, and includes a title and labels on the poster

3—titles and labels poster with limited examples of math, or creates a poster with a variety of math, but does not title or label the poster

2—creates a theme poster with limited math examples and no title or labels

1—attempts to complete the task, but attempt is incorrect (for example, the poster has no theme or does not contain examples of math that relate to the theme)

0—makes no attempt, or attempt is off-task

Newspaper Number Search

Think about all the ways you saw numbers in the newspaper. Write a sentence or two about what you learned. Then write a couple sentences that summarize something you learned about numbers from the newspaper number search.

_____

_____

_____

_____

_____

Brainstorm a few ways that your life would be different if there were no numbers. Write about it below. Then illustrate one idea of how your life would change or be different without numbers.

_____

_____

_____

_____

_____

17 **5** **3**

4 **12** **7**

The Math Problem

Think about the ways you use numbers every day.

Imagine that you had a math "problem"—you did not understand math.

Write about four problems you might have had.

Problem 1: _____

_____

_____

Problem 2: _____

_____

_____

Problem 3: _____

_____

_____

Problem 4: _____

_____

_____

Name _____

Math All Around Us

Choose a theme for a math poster. The ideas in the box will help you.

sports	television
baseball	music
soccer	ballet
football	recipes/cooking
bowling	restaurants
tennis	fast food
basketball	board games
math at the mall	grocery shopping
video games	doctor's visits

What is your theme? _____

Predict where you might see mathematics. Write your ideas below.

1. _____   6. _____
2. _____   7. _____
3. _____   8. _____
4. _____   9. _____
5. _____   10. _____

Now search for examples of mathematics that fit your theme.

Collect examples to display on a poster.

Remember! Math is more than numbers! It includes shapes and angles, probability, money, fractions, patterns, decimals, and measurement. Try to think of all the ways that math relates to your topic.

Real-World Number Problems

Solve these real-world number problems.

Example:

States in the U.S. minus the hours in a day.

50 − 24 = 26

1. Wheels on a tricycle times the planets in our solar system   =   ?

   _____   _____   _____   =   _____

2. Yards on a football field divided by the dimes in a dollar   =   ?

   _____   _____   _____   =   _____

3. Holes on a golf course plus the innings in a baseball game   =   ?

   _____   _____   _____   =   _____

4. Eggs in a dozen divided by the leaves on a shamrock   =   ?

   _____   _____   _____   =   _____

5. Sides on a cube plus seconds in a minute   =   ?

   _____   _____   _____   =   _____

Now write a few "real-world" number problems of your own.
Exchange your problems with a classmate.

1._____

2._____

3._____

4._____

5._____

How I Used Math Today

Think about your day.

How have you used math?

Write about the ways you used math on the lines below.

1. _____
   _____

2. _____
   _____

3. _____
   _____

4. _____
   _____

5. _____
   _____

6. _____
   _____

7. _____
   _____

8. _____
   _____

9. _____
   _____

10. _____
    _____

Restaurants, whether dining in or carrying out, provide plenty of opportunities to explore real-world math. Whether it be totaling a check, deciding on the best value, or figuring out order combinations, students can practice hands-on math in many ways. The following activities require students to investigate the math involved in dining out.

MATH SKILLS CHART

Dining Out Math Skills Chart	Problem Solving	Reasoning/Logic	Communication	Connections	Numeration	Whole Number Operations	Measurement	Data Analysis	Geometry	Rationals (Fractions/Decimals)	Probability/Statistics	Patterns
Food-and-Fun Family Rest.	x	x	x	x	x	x	x			x		x
Video-Game Change	x	x	x	x								
Buying Bagels	x	x	x	x	x	x				x		
Bagel Possibilities	x	x	x	x								
Bagel Glyph	x	x	x	x		x	x	x	x	x		
Home-Style Family Rest.	x	x	x	x	x	x		x		x		
Burger Barn Design Contest	x	x	x	x			x		x			
Grand Opening Celebration	x	x	x	x		x	x					
Burger Barn Problem Solving	x	x	x	x		x				x		
How Many Should You Order?	x	x	x	x		x				x		

USING THE PAGES

Food-and-Fun Family Restaurant (page 18)

Hold a brief discussion about kids' menus at local restaurants. How do the foods and portions differ from adult entrees? How do the prices differ? Then pass out the activity sheet. Instruct students to analyze the information on the menu at the top of the page as they figure out the best value.

Video-Game Change (page 19)

Remind students that some child-oriented restaurants have video games. How much do video games cost? Pass out the activity sheet. Challenge students to come up with coin combinations, using only dimes and nickels, for a 50¢ video game.

Buying Bagels (pages 20–21)

Ahead of time, reproduce and pass out the menu for "Buddy's Bagels" on page 20. Invite students to study the menu, initiating discussion if you wish. Then challenge students to solve the bagel-related math problems on page 21. Remind them to refer to the menu to guide their answers.

Bagel Possibilities (page 22)

Once again using the bagel menu, encourage students to diagram the different bagel-and-topping combinations they could order from "Buddy's Bagels."

Bagel Glyph (page 23)

As a final bagel activity, ask students to create glyphs to show their own bagel preferences. You might create your own bagel glyph so students can visualize the completed project. The first part of the glyph is the most tricky. Students will need a math compass to help them create the initial bagel circle. Once students have completed their glyphs, display them on a bulletin board. Encourage students to analyze the data the glyphs provide to determine the various bagels their classmates prefer.

Home-Style Family Restaurant (page 24)

Talk with students about how a buffet differs from a normal restaurant—that diners usually eat a variety of foods for one price. Depending on the number of people in their families, invite students to figure out how much a breakfast buffet would cost, according to the information on the activity sheet.

Burger Barn Design Contest (pages 25–26)

Let students design their own layouts for a fast-food restaurant. Reproduce and pass out the instructions and the grid. Challenge students to design the restaurant following the specifications and marking the placement on the grid. Suggest that students color-code their designs with different crayons, markers, or colored pencils.

Grand Opening Celebration (page 27)

Have students use their knowledge of elapsed time to create an entertainment schedule for the opening of a fast-food restaurant. Remind them that shows should not overlap.

Burger Barn Problem Solving (page 28)

As students review the activity sheet, point out the menu at the top of the page. Challenge them to solve the math problems by using the data on the menu. As they work, encourage them to consider real-life experiences when these math problems might come into play.

How Many Should You Order? (page 29)

Invite students to place a restaurant order based on a class of 30 students. Explain that they need to figure out the number of students suggested by the fraction. This is the number they write under "quantity." Make sure students' numbers correspond to the food that's ordered.

LITERATURE CONNECTIONS

Math Fun with Money Puzzlers by Rose Wyler presents math concepts through playful money puzzles.

The Story of Money by Betsy Maestro covers the history of money from ancient times to modern monetary systems.

REAL-WORLD MATERIALS

Restaurant menus are great for math activities. Check with local restaurants for "throw-aways" or even take-out menus. Using the menus, let students select a meal and calculate its cost. Older students can include sales tax and a 15% tip. You might also specify an amount of money for students to spend, then ask students to calculate their change after eating. Students can also create class graphs showing the costs of meals, and older students might calculate the mean, median, mode, and range of meal prices.

ASSESSMENT SUGGESTION

Task: *Home-Style Family Restaurant*

Expected Student Outcomes

- creates an accurate table showing name, age, and cost for each family member correctly
- calculates the total cost of the breakfast
- explains the process for calculating the total cost

Scoring Rubric

4—responds correctly to all of the above outcomes

3—responds correctly to at least two of the above outcomes

2—responds correctly to one of the outcomes

1—attempts to complete the problem, but attempt is incorrect

0—makes no attempt, or attempt is off-task

Food-and-Fun Family Restaurant

Read the menu below.

KIDS' MENU

Hot dog and fries ....$1.85   Pizza and fries...........................$1.99

Grilled cheese and fries ....$1.85   Chicken and fries......................$2.35

Hamburger and fries $2.05

Kids' Meal Deals

Choose any lunch/dinner from the above list and
add your choice of beverage and kids' ice cream for just ....$3.49.

Ice Cream

Junior cone ....99¢

Junior sundae............................$1.75

Milkshake ....99¢

Beverages

Soda...85¢

Milk ....89¢

Hot chocolate ....80¢

Juice ....99¢

(orange, tomato, cranberry)

Are the "Kids' Meal Deals" really a bargain? _____

Explain your answer.

_____

_____

_____

_____

_____

_____

Video-Game Change

Some video games cost 50¢ to play.

You have lots of nickels and dimes, but no quarters.

What combinations of nickels and dimes equal 50¢?

Fill out the table below to show all the possible combinations.

Number of Dimes	Value of Dimes	Number of Nickels	Value of Dimes	Total Value

How many coin combinations made up 50¢? _____

How can you be sure that you did not miss any combinations?

Explain your strategy.

_____

_____

_____

_____

_____

Buddy's Bagels

INDIVIDUAL BAGELS

50¢

HALF DOZEN (6)

$2.99

DOZEN (12)

$4.99

BAGEL VARIETIES

wheat • blueberry • raisin • chocolate chip

TOPPINGS

cream cheese...............add 50¢ per bagel

butter.............add 20¢ per bagel

half-pound tub of cream cheese...............$1.99

DRINKS

coffee...............$1.10

orange juice...............$1.30

milk...............99¢

hot cocoa...............$1.10

hot tea...............95¢

20

Buying Bagels

Read the menu for Buddy's Bagels. Then solve these real-world math problems.

1. You and a friend stop by Buddy's for breakfast. Together you have $5.00. What will you buy? Be sure to include drinks and any toppings.

Item	Price
_____	_____
_____	_____
_____	_____
_____	_____
_____	_____
_____	_____
_____	_____
_____	_____
Total:	_____

2. How much change do you have left? Show how you know.

_____

3. A soccer team is having a special team breakfast and needs 18 bagels. The coach can either buy them individually, by the half dozen, by the dozen, or in some combination. Which would be the cheapest? Explain how you know.

_____
_____
_____
_____
_____

Bagel Possibilities

At Buddy's Bagels, customers can order wheat, blueberry, raisin, or chocolate-chip bagels. The bagels come plain or with cream cheese or butter.

Make a list or a tree diagram below to show the combinations.

How many different bagel/topping combinations are there? _____

Circle the one you would order.

© 1998 Good Apple GA1686

Bagel Glyph

Order a bagel from Buddy's.

Create a bagel glyph by answering the questions.

1. Do you prefer your bagel warm or cold?

	warm	cold
Draw a circle with a radius of:	2" (5 cm)	3" (7.5 cm)

2. Which type of bagel will you buy?

Draw this shape
in the center
of your bagel:

plain	blueberry	raisin	chocolate chip
circle	pentagon	hexagon	octagon

3. Which topping would you like on your bagel?

Draw this many seeds
on your bagel:

none	butter	cream cheese
0	5	10

4. What would you like to drink with your bagel?

juice	milk	hot cocoa	other
orange	yellow	tan	pink

Color your bagel:

Now solve these real-world math problems.

1. How much will your breakfast cost? Show how you know.

_____

_____

2. Switch bagel glyphs with a partner.
   How much will your partner's breakfast cost? Show how you know.

_____

_____

23

Name_____

Home-Style Family Restaurant

Read the menu below.

START YOUR DAY WITH OUR BREAKFAST BUFFET!

Adults..$5.95

Children 12 and under eat for..$2.95

Children 6 and under eat for..99¢

Enjoy

scrambled eggs • hash browns • bacon • sausage • ham • scrapple
sausage gravy • grits • biscuits • muffins • creamed chipped beef
pancakes • fresh seasonal fruits • variety of juices

How much will it cost for your family to eat breakfast at the Home-Style Family Restaurant? Fill in the table to figure it out.

Family Member	Age	Price

Total: _____

© 1998 Good Apple GA1686

Burger Barn Design Contest

A new fast-food restaurant called Burger Barn is being planned. The builders are having a contest for the best restaurant design.

You need to include the following items:

6 trash cans—1 square unit each

6 recycling bins—1 square unit each

self-serve drink area—6 square units

children's play area—28 square units

2 restrooms—8 square units each

8 large tables—6 square units each

10 medium tables—4 square units each

6 small tables—2 square units each

2 kiddie tables—4 square units each

2 entrances—2 units wide each

counter for straws, napkins, and condiments—4 square units

Use the grid on page 26 to design the restaurant. Think about a good location for each item. Label them, or provide a color code. Be creative, but be logical, too!

Burger Barn Design Grid

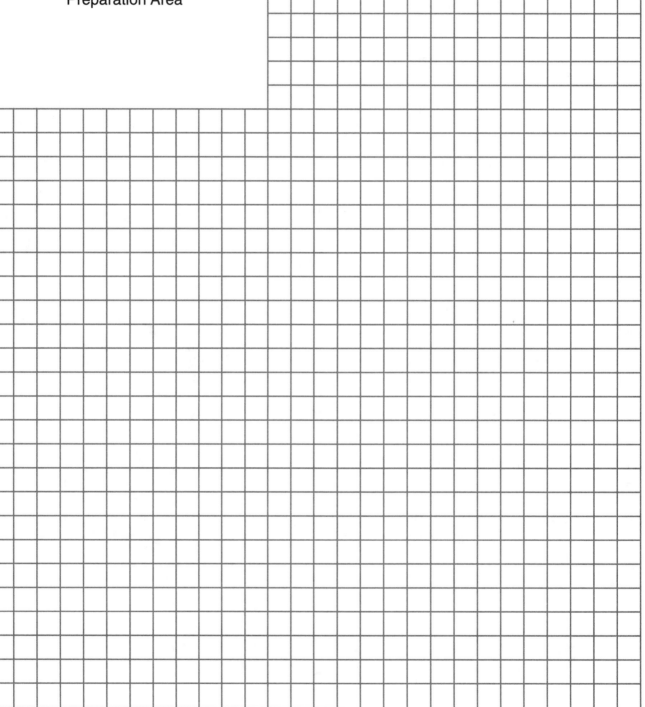

Kitchen/Food

Preparation Area

© 1998 Good Apple GA1686

Name _____

Grand Opening Celebration

A special opening-day celebration is being planned for Burger Barn. Beginning at 2:00, five shows will be performed. Four shows and the amount of time each show takes are listed below. You decide on the fifth show for the celebration.

Write the name of the show and its duration (the amount of time it will take) on the lines.

Celebration Activities!

Comedy Act—35 minutes

Juggling Act—25 minutes

Magic Show—40 minutes

Amazing Animals Act—45 minutes

_____ — _____ minutes

Now plan a schedule for the day's events, choosing the order of the shows. Beginning with the first show at 2:00, write each show on a line. Fill in each clock with the time that the show begins. Remember that the shows run consecutively, one after the other.

 _____

 _____

 _____

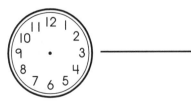 _____

What time will the last show end? _____

Reproducible

Burger Barn Problem Solving

Read the Burger Barn menu below.

MAIN ITEMS

hamburger.................................59¢   cheeseburger ....69¢

chicken nuggets ....$2.09   French fries ....89¢

DRINKS

soft drinks

(cola, lemon-lime, root beer) ....89¢

milk...79¢

milkshake................................99¢

DESSERTS

sundae

(chocolate, strawberry)..........89¢

cookies ....39¢

cherry pie ....79¢

Now solve these real-world math problems.

1. Brendan ordered a cheeseburger, French fries, and a milkshake. How much money did he spend? Explain how you know.

   _____

2. Maria had $4.00. After buying chicken nuggets and a soda, how much did she have left? Explain how you know.

   _____

3. Kate spent half of her money on lunch. Then she spent 79¢ on dessert. She had $1.58 left. How much money did Kate start with? Explain how you know.

   _____

4. What did Kate have for desert? How do you know?

   _____

5. What do you think Kate might have ordered for lunch?

   _____

Show how you know.

28

How Many Should You Order?

Your class is ordering lunch from Burger Barn. There are 30 students in your class. This is what they want:

$\frac{2}{3}$ of them want French fries

$\frac{1}{6}$ ordered hamburgers

$\frac{1}{3}$ want chicken nuggets

$\frac{1}{2}$ would like cheeseburgers

$\frac{2}{5}$ prefer a cola

$\frac{1}{5}$ would like rootbeer

$\frac{2}{5}$ want milk

$\frac{1}{3}$ of the class would like a chocolate sundae

(but $\frac{1}{2}$ of them don't want nuts on it!)

$\frac{1}{5}$ would like a cherry pie

$\frac{2}{5}$ would like chocolate-chip cookies

How many of each food will you order?

Use the table below to list the class order.

OUR CLASS' ORDER

Quantity	Food

29

In the Kitchen

Whether developing shopping lists, estimating the cost of groceries, preparing recipes, or planning family meals, activities in the kitchen lend themselves to numerous math explorations. Ahead of time, collect a variety of kitchen-related materials such as grocery-store ads, nutrition labels, and recipe cards. (See Real-World Materials in this section.)

MATH SKILLS CHART

In the Kitchen Math Skills Chart	Problem Solving	Reasoning/Logic	Communication	Connections	Numeration	Whole Number Operations	Measurement	Data Analysis	Geometry	Rationals (Fractions/Decimals)	Probability/Statistics	Patterns
Sold by the Pound	x	x	x	x		x	x			x		x
Shopping List	x	x	x	x	x	x	x			x		
Super Snack Mix	x	x	x	x		x	x			x		
Snack Riddles	x	x	x	x	x	x				x		
Create a Snack Mix	x	x	x	x	x					x		
Rating Snacks	x	x	x	x		x					x	
The Cookie Sheet	x	x	x	x	x			x			x	

USING THE PAGES

Sold by the Pound (pages 32–33)

Elicit from students foods they know that are sold by the pound. List their ideas on the chalkboard. Encourage them to write their own ideas on the activity sheet. Pass around grocery-store ads for more ideas. You can also reproduce "The Corner Market" coupons on page 33. Then challenge students to calculate the costs per pound at the bottom of the activity sheet.

Shopping List (page 34)

Encourage students to take the activity sheet home to complete with a family member. Explain that they are to estimate how much money they should bring to the grocery in order to purchase the foods listed on the page. Then they figure out the actual cost of the food. Have students and family members write their own shopping lists.

Super Snack Mix (page 35)

As students work with the snack-mix recipe on this page, they will practice and sharpen their fraction, measurement, and reasoning skills.

Snack Riddles (page 36)

Challenge students to solve the snack riddles on this page by drawing upon their logic and number sense. Students may benefit from using real snack foods as manipulatives. Or, ask students to help you create snack-food manipulatives by cutting out various shapes from construction paper. Culminate by asking students to come up with their own snack riddles for classmates to solve.

Create a Snack Mix (page 37)

By creating their own snack mixes, students are asked to determine percentages and ratios of the various snack ingredients. After students follow the sample snack recipe, encourage them to write a recipe for someone at home to follow.

Rating Snacks (pages 38–39)

Which snacks do adults prefer? Which snacks do children prefer? This is what students are asked to discover as they conduct the snack survey on these two pages. Instruct students to rank the snacks according to the data they collect.

The Cookie Sheet (pages 40–41)

Invite students to analyze cookies for fat and sugar content to determine which are healthiest. On page 40, ask students to plot their findings on a double bar graph. On page 41, have students analyze the data to draw conclusions. Students will need nutrition labels from a variety of cookies, as well as colored pencils if they choose to color-code the bar graph.

In the Kitchen

LITERATURE CONNECTIONS

Math Chef: Over 60 Recipes for Kids by Joan D'Amico and Karen Eich-Drummond and *Kids Cook! Fabulous Food for the Whole Family* by Sara and Zachary Williamson are two of several good cookbooks for children that include tips on safety, measurement, and nutrition, and offer a variety of fun-to-prepare recipes.

REAL-WORLD MATERIALS

Grocery-store ads provide prices, measurements, and quantities that can jump-start a variety of problem-solving activities. Have students compile shopping lists, strengthen division skills by calculating unit prices to determine the best deals, and plan meals by choosing foods from the ads. Students can also order items from the least to the most expensive. Coupons can be added to determine extra savings.

Recipes, particularly recipes for foods with "kid" appeal, offer opportunities to work with measurements and fractions. Changing recipes to serve more or less people provides students with multiplication and division practice. The need for an oven or stovetop limits the ability to cook with students. Creating snack mixes is a good option. With snack mixes, students still get the experience of measuring different quantities. And because the amount of each item is arbitrary, it will not affect the final product.

Nutrition labels are another good source for math data. Foods can be compared for fat, calorie, or sugar content. Let students analyze the label data to select balanced meals.

ASSESSMENT SUGGESTION

Task: *The Cookie Sheet*

Expected Student Outcomes

- accurately completes table with sugar and fat data
- creates a double bar graph, including title, labeling of axes, and identifying the two variables
- draws reasonable conclusions about healthiness of cookies based on data

Scoring Rubric

4—responds correctly to all three outcomes

3—responds correctly to two of the three outcomes

2—accurately completes either table or graph

1—attempts to complete the table or graph, but attempt is incorrect

0—makes no attempt, or attempt is off-task

Name_____

Sold by the Pound

Which foods can you think of that are sold by the pound?
Brainstorm some foods and write them below.
Check grocery ads for more items to add to your list.

_____

_____   _____

_____   _____

_____   _____

_____   _____

Why do you think these foods are sold by the pound?

_____

_____

_____

Choose a food from a grocery ad that is sold by the pound. Complete the table below to show the cost for 1, 2, 3, 4, and 5 pounds.

Item _____

Pounds	1	2	3	4	5
Cost					

Items do not always weigh an even number of pounds. Calculate the cost of these weights for your food.

1.2 pounds = _____ (cost)   4.7 pounds = _____ (cost)

2.6 pounds = _____ (cost)   5.9 pounds = _____ (cost)

3.4 pounds = _____ (cost)

32

Name_____

The Corner Market

 Green Beans
88¢/lb.

 Extra-Large Cooked Shrimp
$11.99/lb.

 Soft Drinks (12-pack)
$2.49

 Eggs (1 dozen)
$1.09

 Sausage
$2.19/lb.

 Grapefruit
2 for $1.00

 Orange Juice ($\frac{1}{2}$ gallon)
$2.47

 Cookies (12-oz. pkg.)
$2.55

 Apples
85¢/lb.

 Jelly Beans
$1.59/lb.

 Cereal (15-oz. box)
$2.99

 Milk (1 gallon)
$2.69

 Strawberries
.99¢/lb.

 Macaroni Salad
$1.99/lb.

 Peanuts
69¢/lb.

 Sliced Ham
$3.99/lb.

 Bacon (1-lb. pkg.)
$3.29

 Potato Chips (14-oz. bag)
$1.98

 Ice Cream ($\frac{1}{2}$ gallon)
$3.29

 Chocolate Cake
$5.99

 Bagels (pkg. of 6)
$1.49

 Cheese Pizza
$3.49

33

Name_____

Shopping List

Challenge someone in your family in this estimation game. Look at the shopping list below. Estimate how much money you will need. Use "The Corner Market" coupons for prices.

2 lbs. green beans
1 gal. milk
1 box cereal
3 lbs. peanuts
1 grapefruit

Name_____

Estimate_____

Name_____

Estimate_____

Now, together, calculate the exact cost of the foods on the list.

2 lbs. green beans = _____

1 gallon milk = _____

1 box cereal = _____

3 lbs. peanuts = _____

1 grapefruit = _____

Total = _____

How close were you to the actual cost? _____

How close was your family member to the actual cost? _____

Whose estimate was closer? _____

Now make your own shopping list.
Look through grocery ads from the newspaper at home. Try your estimation skills again. Write your list, estimates, and total cost on the back of this page.

© 1998 Good Apple GA1686

Super Snack Mix

Read the recipe below for making Super Snack Mix.

Super Snack Mix

Mix together:

1 cup dry cereal	8 mini-pretzels
$\frac{1}{2}$ cup marshmallows	$\frac{3}{4}$ cup peanuts
$\frac{1}{3}$ cup raisins	$\frac{2}{3}$ cup chocolate chips

Serves 1 dozen people.

Now solve these real-world math problems.

1. Your family has a party. Sixty people show up! How much snack mix should you make? Explain how you know.

_____

2. How many batches of Super Snack Mix will you need to serve your whole class? Show how you know.

_____

3. Rewrite the recipe to show the amounts of each ingredient you will need in order to serve everyone in your class.

_____ cereal

_____ marshmallows

_____ raisins

_____ pretzels

_____ peanuts

_____ chocolate chips

35

Snack Riddles

Solve these snack-mix riddles.

1. There are six raisins. There are twice as many pretzels as raisins. There are half as many peanuts as raisins. How many of each food are there?

   pretzels _____   peanuts _____   raisins _____

2. The number of raisins is double the number of peanuts. There is one less pretzel than raisin. There are 24 pieces in all. How many of each food are there?

   pretzels _____   peanuts _____   raisins _____

3. The number of pretzels and raisins is the same. There are three more peanuts than the number of pretzels and raisins combined. There are 19 pieces in all. How many of each food are there?

   pretzels _____   peanuts _____   raisins _____

4. There are four fewer pretzels than raisins. There are half as many peanuts as raisins. There are 16 pieces in all. How many of each food are there?

   pretzels _____   peanuts _____   raisins _____

5. There are three times as many peanuts as raisins. There are 5 pretzels. There are 25 pieces in all. How many of each food are there?

   pretzels _____   peanuts _____   raisins _____

Now make up your own snack riddle for someone else to solve.

_____

_____

_____

_____

36

Create a Snack Mix

Make some snack mixes of your own. Follow these instructions.

1. Make a peanut, raisin, and pretzel snack mix.

   The snack mix should contain 20 pieces of food:

   $\frac{1}{5}$ raisins, $\frac{3}{10}$ peanuts, and $\frac{1}{2}$ pretzels.

   How many of each food is in your mix?

   pretzels _____   peanuts _____   raisins _____

   What percentage of the mix is raisins? _____

   What percentage of the mix is peanuts? _____

   What percentage of the mix is pretzels? _____

2. Make a snack mix using 24 pieces:

   $\frac{1}{6}$ raisins, $\frac{1}{2}$ peanuts, and $\frac{1}{3}$ pretzels.

   How many of each food is in your mix?

   pretzels _____   peanuts _____   raisins _____

   What is the ratio of raisins to peanuts? _____

   What is the ratio of pretzels to raisins? _____

   What is the ratio of peanuts to pretzels? _____

Now you try it!

Write a similar recipe for someone else to follow to make a snack mix.

_____

_____

_____

_____

_____

_____

_____

Rating Snacks

Do adults and children like the same snacks? Collect data to find out.

STEP 1

Which snacks do **you** like? Rate the snacks on a 1 to 5 scale, with 1 being the highest and 5 being the lowest. Some snacks may have the same rating.

My Ratings of Each Snack

1. popcorn	1	2	3	4	5
2. ice cream	1	2	3	4	5
3. candy	1	2	3	4	5
4. vegetables and dip	1	2	3	4	5
5. fruit	1	2	3	4	5
6. cookies	1	2	3	4	5

STEP 2

Now ask an **adult** to rate the snacks in the same way.

Adult Ratings of Each Snack

1. popcorn	1	2	3	4	5
2. ice cream	1	2	3	4	5
3. candy	1	2	3	4	5
4. vegetables and dip	1	2	3	4	5
5. fruit	1	2	3	4	5
6. cookies	1	2	3	4	5

Bring your data to class tomorrow.

© 1998 Good Apple GA1686

Rating Snacks

STEP 3

Work in groups of 4 or 5 students. On the back of this page, write the data your classmates gathered. Then find the averages for each snack, for both children and adults. Round each average to the nearest tenth. Write the averages below.

AVERAGE RATINGS

Children		Adults	
Snack #1 _____	Snack #4 _____	Snack #1 _____	Snack #4 _____
Snack #2 _____	Snack #5 _____	Snack #2 _____	Snack #5 _____
Snack #3 _____	Snack #6 _____	Snack #3 _____	Snack #6 _____

STEP 4

Now rank the snacks from the most liked to the least liked.

Children's Rankings	Adults' Rankings
1.	1.
2.	2.
3.	3.
4.	4.
5.	5.
6.	6.

STEP 5

What conclusions can you draw about this information? Use mathematical data to support your answer.

_____

_____

_____

The Cookie Sheet

Do you think all cookies have the same amount of sugar and fat? Follow these steps to find out.

STEP 1

Read the nutrition labels on six different cookie packages. Write your findings in the table below.

Cookie	Sugar (grams)	Fat (grams)

STEP 2

Now prepare a double bar graph for the data from your table. Use a different color or line for sugar and fat. Remember to title your graph and label both axes.

_____

40

The Cookie Sheet

STEP 3

Now analyze the data on your graph.

1. Which cookie do you think is the most healthy to eat? Explain your answer.

_____

_____

_____

2. Which cookie do you think is the least healthy to eat? Explain your answer.

_____

_____

_____

3. Write a letter to a friend. Tell your friend which cookie would make the healthiest snack and which cookie they should avoid. Explain the math data you discovered.

_____

_____

_____

_____

_____

_____

_____

_____

_____

_____

41

Sports

The world of sports is filled with math, from daily game statistics reported in newspapers to schedules and scoring; from the sizes and shapes of playing fields to the cost of participating in or attending sporting events. The following activities capitalize on students' interest in sports.

MATH SKILLS CHART

Sports Math Skills Chart	Problem Solving	Reasoning/Logic	Communication	Connections	Numeration	Whole Number Operations	Measurement	Data Analysis	Geometry	Rationals (Fractions/Decimals)	Probability/Statistics	Patterns
Comparing Baseball Players	x	x	x	x	x			x				
How Tall Are They?	x	x	x	x	x	x	x	x			x	
Through the Years	x	x	x	x				x		x	x	
Baseball Glyph	x	x	x	x			x	x	x	x		
Batting Averages Bar Graph	x	x	x	x	x	x		x		x	x	
Most Valuable Player	x	x	x	x	x	x		x			x	
Ballpark Birthday	x	x	x	x			x			x		
Picnic at the Ballpark	x	x	x	x		x		x		x		
Plotting the Hits	x	x	x	x				x				
Bowling Tournament	x	x	x	x	x	x					x	
Scoring Baskets	x	x	x	x	x					x		
Home or Away?	x	x	x	x		x		x			x	x

USING THE PAGES

Baseball Abbreviations (page 44)

As students work through the baseball-related math activities, they will come across many common baseball abbreviations. Reproduce and pass out this page as a reference to guide students as they analyze baseball data.

Comparing Baseball Players (page 45)

Have students work in pairs to complete this activity sheet. Instruct each student to choose a baseball card and to jot down information about the player on the chart. Have students record each other's player information, too. Then ask them to compare the players by following the directions.

How Tall Are They? (page 46)

Help students find the average height of a group of baseball players. First, remind them how to convert feet (or meters) and inches (or centimeters) to inches (or centimeters) only. Working in groups of four to five, have students record their measurements on the stem-and-leaf chart. Then have them figure out the average height, median, mode, and range.

Through the Years (page 47)

Invite students to choose a baseball card. Point out the number that shows the player's yearly batting average. Challenge students to plot the average on a graph. Explain that they are also to determine the X and Y axis for the grid. Encourage them to analyze their data.

Baseball Glyph (pages 48–49)

Encourage students to use data from a baseball card to create a glyph. You might create your own glyph so students can see the finished product. Start by showing students how to cut out the correct-sized circle for their players, using a math compass and a ruler. As students work, create a bar graph on mural paper. You will need five headings, one for each range on the activity sheet. Let students make their own graphs on the grid on page 49.

Most Valuable Player (page 50)

Let students work in groups to determine a "most valuable player" among the baseball cards. Have students first compute points for their own players, following the directions on the page. Then ask students to rank the baseball players in the group according to the points scored.

Sports

Ballpark Birthday (pages 51–53)

Reproduce the Baseball Brochure on page 51 for students to use with the activity sheets on pages 52 and 53. Invite students to choose a baseball game to attend, according to the schedule on the brochure. Have them answer the remaining questions to plan their parties. Also ask students to plan a picnic at the ballpark, listing the guests who will attend and the total cost.

Plotting the Hits (page 54)

Challenge students to analyze plots on a graph to answer questions about a baseball game. Review the baseball diamond, ensuring that all students understand the layout and positions. Then explain that these are the places where the balls landed. Ask them to write the coordinates for each play.

Bowling Tournament (page 55)

Instruct students to find the average bowling score for each player to determine the group winner.

Scoring Baskets (page 56)

Share with students the various ways to score points during a basketball game, as described on the activity sheet. Then ask students to list all the point combinations that would make up nine points during the game.

Home or Away? (pages 57–58)

Invite students to complete this activity at home over several days. Explain that they are to choose a team and record the team's scores for both home and away games. Later, they will analyze the data in class to determine if the team has a better winning percentage at home or on the road.

LITERATURE CONNECTIONS

Sports Math Mania! by Lorraine Jean Hopping and Christopher Egan includes many major sports and helps students understand sports statistics. It also includes sports trivia and wacky facts.

Sports Illustrated for Kids, the monthly sports magazine published by *Sports Illustrated*, also contains sports data on current sports figures and current sporting events.

REAL-WORLD MATERIALS

The newspaper is filled with daily sports statistics for both local and national teams.

Sports trading cards can be useful math props and are available for many sports, including baseball, football, hockey, and basketball. They include a variety of math statistics.

ASSESSMENT SUGGESTION

Task: *Through the Years*

Expected Student Outcomes

- selects accurate data from a baseball card
- correctly creates a line graph, including a title and labeled axes
- able to interpret graph data to answer questions and draw conclusions

Scoring Rubric

4—selects accurate data, creates an accurate graph, and is able to answer questions and draw conclusions using the graph

3—selects accurate data and creates an accurate line graph

2—selects accurate data from card

1—attempts to complete the graph, but the response is incorrect

0—makes no attempt, or attempt is off-task

Baseball Abbreviations

The abbreviations below are used in baseball. Use these abbreviations to help you understand the baseball information you find in newspapers and on baseball cards.

G	number of games played
AB	number of times at bat
R	number of runs scored
H	number of hits
2B	number of doubles hit
3B	number of triples hit
HR	number of home runs hit
SB	number of stolen bases
BB	number of walks (base on balls)
RBI	number of runs batted in
AVG	batting average (number of hits divided by number of times at bat)
ERA	earned run average for a pitcher

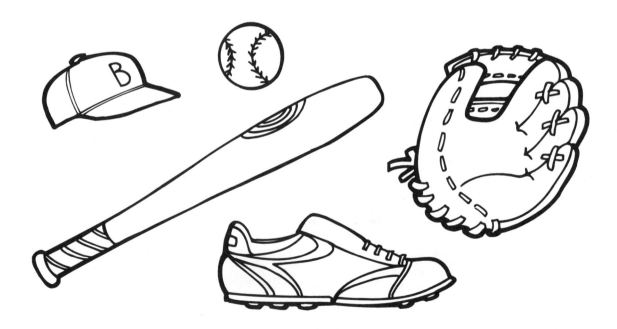

Comparing Baseball Players

Work with a partner to compare baseball players. Each student selects a baseball card. With your partner, complete lines one through four on the table using the data from the baseball cards. Be sure to write the players' names on the chart, too.

Statistic	Player #1_____	Player #2_____
Height		
Weight		
Career Batting Average		
Career Home Runs		

Using the table, compare your and your partner's data.

1. Draw a circle around the height of the tallest player.
2. Draw a box around the weight of the heaviest player.
3. Draw two lines under the highest batting average.
4. Draw a star next to the greatest number of career home runs.

Look at your baseball cards again. Find three more ways to compare your players and add these to your table. Circle the higher number for each piece of data.

Reproducible

How Tall Are They?

Find out the average height for a group of baseball players. Follow these steps.

STEP 1

1. Select a baseball card. Write the player's height here:

   The player is _____ feet (or meters) and _____ inches

   (or centimeters) tall.

2. Convert the height into inches (or centimeters) only. Explain how you do it.

   _____

   The player is _____ inches (or centimeters) tall.

STEP 2

With a group or the whole class, record all the players' heights in inches (or centimeters) on this stem-and-leaf chart. Remember—on a stem-and-leaf chart, the tens digit is in the left column (the stem), and the ones digit is in the right column (the leaves). For example, for the data *23, 25, 26,* and *26,* the stem would be *2* and the leaves would be *3, 5, 6, 6.*

HEIGHTS OF BASEBALL PLAYERS

stem	leaves
0	
1	
2	
3	
4	
5	
6	
7	
8	
9	

STEP 3

Now analyze the data you collected.

1. What is the mean (average) height?_____ inches (centimeters)

2. Explain how you know: _____

3. Convert the average height to feet (or meters) and inches (or centimeters):

   The average height was _____ feet (or meters) and _____ inches

   (or centimeters).

46

Through the Years

Read the yearly batting average on the back of a player's baseball card. Record the data on a line graph. Make sure your player has played for at least five years.

Write a title for your graph, and label the x and y axes.

_____
(title)

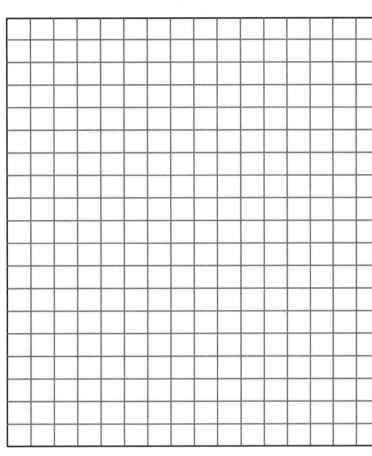

Now analyze your graph.

1. In which year did the player have the best average? _____

2. In which year was his average the worst? _____

3. What trends do you see in the player's batting?

_____

_____

_____

Name_____

Baseball Glyph

Create a baseball glyph by answering the questions. Use the information on a baseball card.

1. Does the player throw with his right hand or left hand?

	right	left
size of ball	4" diameter (10 cm)	5" diameter (12.5 cm)

2. Does the player bat right-handed or left-handed?

	right	left
stitching	⚾ single line	⚾ double line

3. What is the player's height?

	under 6 feet (2 meters)	over 6 feet (2 meters)
number of notches on each stitch	⚾ 4	⚾ 5

4. What is the player's career batting average?

	0–.199	.200–.249	.250–.299	.300–.349	.350 +
color of ball	yellow	green	orange	blue	red

Analyze your classmates' glyphs to create a bar graph with your class.

Batting Averages Bar Graph

Use the grid below to create your own bar graph of batting averages. Refer to the bar graph the class created, or collect data from your classmates. Remember to title and label your graphs.

_____

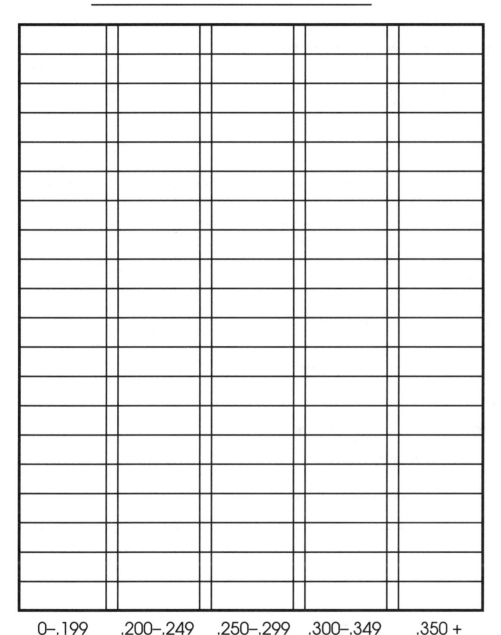

| 0–.199 | .200–.249 | .250–.299 | .300–.349 | .350 + |

What conclusions can you draw from the graph?

_____

_____

Name_____

Most Valuable Player

Work with a group to select the most valuable player.
Give a baseball card to each member of the group.
Then follow the steps below.

STEP 1

Calculate the points for **your** player.

Category	# points for each one		# for my player		Total points for this category
HR (home runs)	4	x		=	
3B (triples)	3	x		=	
2B (doubles)	2	x		=	
1B (singles)	1	x		=	
Runs	1	x		=	
RBI (runs batted in)	1	x		=	

Total Points Earned:

STEP 2

Now work with your group to rank the players.

Group Rankings (from best to worst)

1._____

2._____

3._____

4._____

5._____

6._____

STEP 3

Our group's Most Valuable Player is _____ because

_____

© 1998 Good Apple GA1686

Baseball Brochure

 BATTERRRR . . . UP!

This summer there's a new game in town—minor league baseball. Good food, great seats, giveaways, and more are in store for you!

Ticket Information

	Adults	Children (6–12) Seniors (60 and up)	Children (5 and under)
General Admission	$5.00	$3.00	FREE
Box Seats	$7.00	$7.00	FREE

PICNICS AT THE PARK

Enjoy an all-you-can-eat buffet during the game from your seat immediately behind home plate. Menu includes: hamburgers, hot dogs, salads, dessert, and soft drinks. The following prices include the cost of game tickets and the buffet: $15.00 Adults, $13.00 children (6–12) and seniors, $10.00 children (3–5), children 2 and under free. Limited to groups of ten or more.

SEASON SCHEDULE

June

SUN	MON	TUES	WED	THUR	FRI	SAT
						1 FAY 7PM
2 FAY 2PM	3 CWV	4 CWV	5 CWV	6 HAG	7 HAG	8 GRE
9 GRE	10 GRE	11 GRE	12 AUG 7PM	13 AUG 7PM	14 AUG 7PM	15 AUG 7PM
16 OFF	17 ALL STAR	18 OFF	19 CWV 7PM	20 CWV 7PM	21 CWV 7PM	22 CWV 7PM
23 HIC 2PM	24 HIC 7PM	25 HIC 7PM	26 HIC 12:30	27 HAG 7PM	28 HAG 7PM	29/30 HAG 7PM

July

SUN	MON	TUES	WED	THUR	FRI	SAT
	1 ASH	2 ASH	3 ASH	4 ASH	5 CWV	6 CWV
7 CWV	8 CWV	9 OFF	10 FAY 7PM	11 FAY 7PM	12 FAY 7PM	13 FAY 7PM
14 PIE 7PM	15 PIE 7PM	16 PIE 7PM	17 PIE 7PM	18 OFF	19 HAG 7PM	20 HAG
21 HAG 2PM	22 HAG 7PM	23 GRE 7PM	24 GRE 12:30	25 GRE 7PM	26 GRE 7PM	27 FAY
28 FAY	29 FAY	30 FAY	31 OFF			

August

SUN	MON	TUES	WED	THUR	FRI	SAT
				1 ASH 7PM	2 ASH 7PM	3 ASH 7PM
4 ASH 2PM	5 FAY 7PM	6 FAY 7PM	7 FAY 7PM	8 FAY 7PM	9 HAG 7PM	10 HAG 7PM
11 HAG	12 HAG	13 PIE	14 PIE	15 PIE	16 PIE	17 FAY
18 FAY	19 FAY	20 FAY	21 GRE 7PM	22 GRE 7PM	23 GRE 7PM	24 GRE 7PM
25 OFF	26 HIC	27 HIC	28 HIC	29 HIC	30 HAG	31 HAG

 home   ☐ away

GIVEAWAYS

SPORTS BAGS....................... JUNE 23	BASEBALL GLOVES................ AUG. 10
BEACH TOWELS...................... JULY 13	BACKPACKS .... AUG. 23
JACKETS.................................. AUG. 3	

Reproducible

Ballpark Birthday

Plan a birthday party at the ballpark! Follow the steps below.
Use the information on the Baseball Brochure to help you.

STEP 1

1. Your birthday is July 12. Which Saturday game is closest to your birthday?

   _____

2. What time does the game begin that day? _____

3. What special giveaways are offered at that game? _____

STEP 2

1. Your uncle brought $18.00. He bought 2 tickets.
   How much did it cost for general admission to the game for you and your uncle?

   _____

2. How much money does he have left? _____

STEP 3

Read the following snack-bar menu.

Popcorn $1.50	Peanuts.....................................$1.00
Cotton Candy $1.25	Hot Dog $1.75
Soft Drinks small $0.85	
large...................$1.25	

1. List the foods you would like and their prices.

   Food   **Price**

   _____   _____

   _____   _____

   _____   _____

   _____   _____

2. What is the total cost of your snacks? _____

3. How much money will your uncle have left? Show how you know.

   _____

© 1998 Good Apple GA1686

Name_____

Picnic at the Ballpark

Plan a picnic with your family and friends at the ballpark.
Read the Baseball Brochure for more information.

1. What is the minimum number of people you can have in your group to get the special "picnic in the park" deal? _____

2. On the chart below, list the names and ages of the people you would like to come to the picnic. Write the price for each guest.

PICNIC GUESTS

Name	Age	Price
1.		
2.		
3.		
4.		
5.		
6.		
7.		
8.		
9.		
10.		

3. What is the total cost for your picnic at the ballpark? _____

Name_____

Plotting the Hits

Look at the grid below. It shows a baseball field. The circles show where some of the baseballs landed.

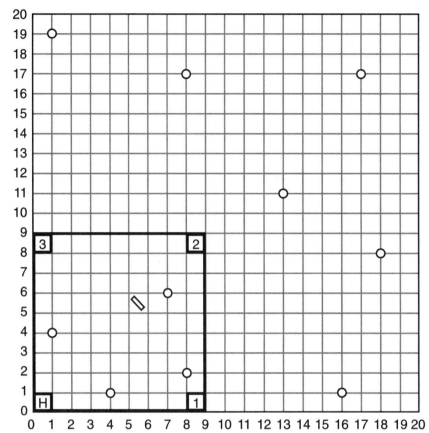

Write the coordinates for the hits below.

1. The batter bunted the ball down the third-base line. _____

2. The batter hit the ball way out in left field. It was almost foul! _____

3. The pitcher had to move quickly to avoid getting hit with the ball.

   _____

4. The first baseman caught the ball. _____

5. The first baseman watched this one sail over his head. _____

6. This ball was hit the farthest out in center field. _____

7. Draw in a ball that you think the third baseman might have been able to

   catch. What are the coordinates of the ball? _____

54

Name_____

Bowling Tournament

Look at the bowling scores below. Then answer the questions.

BOWLING TOURNAMENT GAME SCORES

	Game 1	Game 2	Game 3	Average
Kevin	95	95	80	
Melissa	100	90	95	
Michael	90	80	103	

1. The bowler with the best average wins an ice-cream sundae. Who do you think had the best overall average? Circle your estimated answer.

2. Calculate the average score for Kevin. Show how you do it.

_____

_____

Write Kevin's average on the scorecard.

3. Calculate the average score for Melissa. Show how you do it.

_____

_____

Write Melissa's average on the scorecard.

4. Calculate the average score for Michael. Show how you do it.

_____

_____

Write Michael's average on the scorecard.

5. Who won the ice-cream sundae? _____

6. If you bowled 88 and 95 in the first two games, what would you have to bowl in the third game to tie with the winner? _____

Explain your answer on the back of this page.

Reproducible

Scoring Baskets

There are several ways to score points in a
basketball game.

free throw (foul shot) = 1 point

field goal (basket) = 2 points

shot from far out = 3 points

Imagine you helped your basketball team by scoring
9 points. How might you have scored them? Write the point
combinations below. One possibility is already done for you.

POSSIBLE WAYS TO SCORE 9 POINTS

number of 3-point shots	number of 2-point shots	number of 1-point shots
3	0	0

Your team scored 36 points.

What percentage of the points did you score? _____

Show how you know.

_____

Home or Away?

Sports teams play games at home or in their home stadiums. They also play games away, or at other teams' stadiums. Where does a team play best?

Over several weeks, collect information from television, radio, or a local newspaper on the wins and losses of a local team. The more games the team has played, the better your data will be, so pick a sport that plays frequently, such as baseball, hockey, or basketball.

Record your information on the chart below.

Team Name: _____   **Sport:** _____

RECORD OF TEAM WINS AND LOSSES

Game Date	Home or Away?	Win or Loss?

TEAM GAME SUMMARY

Games	Number of Games Won	Number of Games Lost	Total Number of Games
Played at Home			
Played Away			

Home or Away?

Now analyze your data.

1. What is the percentage of games won by your team?
   Divide the number of games won by the number of games played.
   That will give you the percentage of games won.

   The team's winning percentage was _____ .

2. Find the percentage of wins for home games only. (Remember to use data from home games only.)

   The team's winning percentage at home was _____ .

3. Find the percentage of wins for away games only. (Remember to use data from away games only.)

   The team's winning percentage away was _____ .

Does the team perform better at home or away? Explain your answer.

_____

_____

_____

_____

_____

_____

58

This section deals with interesting activities students might do in their free time. Whether students are traveling with their families, visiting amusement parks or museums, playing games, or planning special events like birthday parties, there are many motivating activities that connect math to the real world.

MATH SKILLS CHART

Travel and Entertainment Math Skills Chart	Problem Solving	Reasoning/Logic	Communication	Connections	Numeration	Whole Number Operations	Measurement	Data Analysis	Geometry	Rationals (Fractions/Decimals)	Probability/Statistics	Patterns
Weather Map Travels	x	x	x	x	x	x	x	x	x		x	
Family Fun Parks	x	x	x	x		x	x	x		x		
Aquarium Adventure	x	x	x	x	x	x				x		
Birthday Plans	x	x	x	x	x	x	x	x	x	x		
Music to Your Ears	x	x	x	x	x	x		x		x		
What Are the Chances?	x	x	x	x							x	
Classroom Games	x	x	x	x		x				x		

USING THE PAGES

Weather Map Travels (pages 61–63)

Invite students to choose a city they would like to visit. Supply them with a national weather map, found in your local newspaper. Talk with students about the map, and point out the weather information. Using the activity sheet on page 61, encourage students to track the weather for their cities, and write the temperatures on the chart. Ask students to display the temperatures on a double line graph. Culminate by having them write a letter to a friend about the city and what they hope to see there. Encourage students to reference encyclopedias and other nonfiction materials to include interesting information about the place as well.

Family Fun Parks (pages 64–66)

Ask students if they have ever been to an amusement park at which prices or rides were determined by height. Pass out the amusement park "brochure" on page 64, and review the information. Explain that students will figure out the price of admission for each person in their families, based on their heights. Have students take home the brochure and the chart on page 65. They can use a tape measure to measure family members' heights.

Aquarium Adventure (page 66)

Ask students to read the information about the aquarium at the top of the page, then challenge them to figure out the price of admission for their entire families. Encourage them to figure out the best value as well.

Birthday Plans (pages 67–70)

Invite students to calculate the cost of a birthday party. On page 68, ask students to choose the party and the number of guests, then figure out the total cost. On page 69, challenge them to arrange snack bags, without exceeding the budget. On page 70, students select their own refreshments, staying within the $30.00 budget. Provide grocery ads or copies of "The Corner Market" coupons on page 33. Finally, on page 70 have students practice geometry skills as they plan party decorations.

Music to Your Ears (page 71)

Let students "cash in" a gift certificate at a local music store. As they list the items they would buy, make sure they include the prices. As an extra challenge, ask them to figure out the suggested 5% sales tax, or share with them the sales tax for your area. Make sure students do not go over $25.00.

Travel and Entertainment

What Are the Chances? (pages 72–73)

Invite students to test probabilities by creating and spinning a "chance" wheel. Show students how to construct the wheel by cutting out the pattern, placing a paper clip in the center, and holding the clip there with a sharpened pencil point. Have students flick the paper clip with a finger to make it move. After they fill in the sections of the wheel, have them complete the probability problems on page 73.

Classroom Games (pages 74–75)

Reproduce the game list on page 75. As students review the list, ask them to imagine that they have been granted $100.00 to spend on new games for their class. Which games would they choose? On the activity sheet, have students list their game choices. Challenge them to stay within the budget. Instruct them to add the prices to determine if they have met this goal.

LITERATURE CONNECTIONS

The Kids' Complete Guide to Money by Kathy S. Kyte presents ideas such as comparison shopping, advertising, and bartering in a fun and creative way.

In *Everything You Need to Survive: Money Problems*, Jane and Bob Stine humorously guide children on how to best manage their money.

REAL-WORLD MATERIALS

Travel brochures are widely available and contain plenty of math data, including admission costs, special rates, times the attractions are open, calendars listing special events, distances to the attractions, and more. Brochures can be obtained by writing to state tourist bureaus, visiting highway rest stations and hotel lobbies, or collecting them at the attractions. Newspapers also contain travel sections that give information about the cost of airfares, hotels, rental cars, and admissions.

Advertisements from toy stores and music stores provide lots of data. Students can select and calculate the cost for items they'd like to purchase, or calculate the sale price for items that are being sold at 20%, 30%, $\frac{1}{2}$ or $\frac{1}{3}$ discounts.

Many activity centers (bowling alleys, roller-skating rinks) have special party brochures with information about party rates.

ASSESSMENT SUGGESTION

Task: *Aquarium Adventure*

Expected Student Outcomes

- accurately records the admission price for each family member
- accurately determines cheaper rate: multiple trips or unlimited price
- justifies answer using math data

Scoring Rubric

4—records accurate prices, determines the cheaper rate, and is able to justify the answer

3—records accurate prices, and accurately determines the cheaper rate

2—records accurate prices, but does not accurately determine the cheapest rate

1—attempts to complete the problem, but responses are incorrect

0—makes no attempt, or attempt is off-task

Name_____

Weather Map Travels

The newspaper provides daily weather information for cities around the world. Think of a city you would like to visit. Gather daily weather data (high and low temperatures) for one week.

City: _____

DAILY WEATHER DATA

	Daily High Temperatures	Daily Low Temperatures
Day 1		
Day 2		
Day 3		
Day 4		
Day 5		
Day 6		
Day 7		

Analyze Your Data

1. Using your weather data, calculate the mean (average) high and low temperatures for the week.

   Mean high temperature: _____   Mean low temperature: _____

   Explain how you got your answer.

   _____

   _____

2. What was the median high temperature? _____

   Explain how you know. _____

   _____

3. What was the range of temperatures for the week? _____

Name _____

Weather Map Travels

Design a double line graph to display your data. Be sure to title your graph and label both axes.

_____
(title)

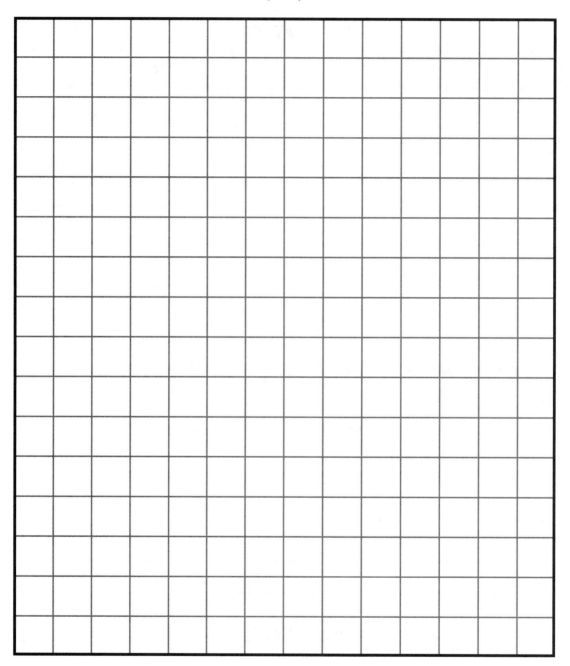

On the back of this page, explain why a double line graph is a good choice to display your weather data.

© 1998 Good Apple GA1686

Weather Map Travels

Research your city using an encyclopedia, reference book, or travel brochure. Read about recreational opportunities there. Think about the activities that would suit the current temperatures.

Imagine that you and a friend will be visiting this city. Write a letter to your friend telling him or her about the weather. Suggest some items to pack for the trip. Mention some recreational activities you might do when you get there.

_____
_____
_____
_____
_____
_____
_____
_____
_____
_____
_____
_____
_____
_____
_____

63

Family Fun Parks

Adventure Mountain Theme Park

More than 100 thrilling rides and attractions!

General Admission — $34.00

Seniors 55 and over — $20.00

Children under 48" (120 cm) in height — $17.00

Children 2 years and under — FREE

Water Adventure Park

Enjoy our wave pool and water slides!

General Admission — $18.00

Seniors 55 years and over — $11.00

Children below 48" (120 cm) in height — $11.00

*Combo ticket for one person to visit both parks — $49.00 *

Name _____

Family Fun Parks

Read the brochure.

Which park would you like to visit with your family?

_____

1. In the chart below, list each family member, his or her height, and admission cost per person.

Name	Height	Cost for Admission

2. What is the total cost for your family? _____

3. If your family decides to go to both parks, who do you think should purchase a combo ticket? Do you think it is a good deal for every member of your family? Justify your answer.

_____

_____

_____

_____

Name_____

Aquarium Adventure

Read the information below.

Enjoy a spectacular journey through one of the largest aquariums in the country. Join us in exploring the underwater mysteries found in the world's oceans.

ADMISSION

Adults: $8.75
Children 2–12 years: $5.75
Children under 2: FREE
Unlimited Annual Family Visits: $60.00

List the ages and admission cost for each family member in the chart below.

Name	Age	Cost of Admission

What is the total cost for your family? _____

The aquarium offers a special rate for unlimited visits to the aquarium. How many times do you think your family would have to visit the aquarium to

make the unlimited admission ticket the best buy? _____

Explain how you know.

_____

_____

66

Birthday Plans

Plan a birthday party. Follow these steps.

Step 1

You invite ten guests to your party. Decide where you will go. Figure out how much your party will cost. Remember to include yourself in the price.

Have a Bowling Party!
$4.50 per person

Have a Miniature Golf Party!
$3.50 per person

Have a Rollerblading Party!
$4.75 per person

I will have a _____ party.

The total cost will be _____ .

Explain below how you figured out the cost of the party.

_____

_____

_____

_____

_____

© 1998 Good Apple GA1686

Souvenir Bags

You would like to give each guest a souvenir bag. But you cannot spend more than $15.00. Decide on the items to fill the bags.

Complete the table to show what you will order. You may order 0 (none) of an item, too. Remember—you will need eleven bags. That includes one for you!

SOUVENIR BAG FILLERS

Item	Package Size	Price	Quantity	Subtotal
Cherry licorice sticks	20 pieces	$3.00		
Striped pencils	1 dozen	$2.00		
Glow-in-the-dark stickers	10 sheets	$2.50		
Silly dough	8 packs	$2.25		
Neon memo pads	6 pads	$3.50		

Total spent on bags: _____

Did you go over or stay under your budget?_____

Explain how you know.

_____

_____

_____

_____

_____

_____

_____

Refreshments

You have $30.00 to spend on party refreshments.

Using grocery ads, decide which foods and drinks you will have.

List the refreshments in the chart, along with the cost and quantity. Remember—there will be 11 guests.

PARTY REFRESHMENTS

Food or Drink	Price	Quantity	Subtotal

Total spent on refreshments: _____

Did you go over or stay under your budget? _____

Explain how you know.

_____

_____

_____

_____

_____

_____

_____

69

Party Decorations

Follow these steps to figure out the decorations for your party.

1. You are in charge of decorating a bulletin board in the party room. The bulletin board is 4 feet (1.2 meters) high and 5 feet (1.5 meters) long. You want to cover the bulletin board with red paper. The paper is sold by the square foot (meter). How much paper will you need?

   _____

   Explain how you figured it out.

   _____

   _____

2. You found a roll of blue ribbon at the store for the border of the board.

   How many feet (or centimeters) of ribbon will you need? _____

   Explain how you figured it out.

   _____

   _____

3. When you get to the check-out, you are told that the ribbon is only sold by the yard. How many yards (or meters) should you buy? _____

   Explain how you figured it out.

   _____

   _____

4. You would like to tape balloons around the border of the board. If you taped one balloon every foot (30 cm), how many balloons would you need?

   _____

   Explain how you figured it out.

   _____

   _____

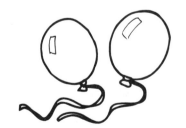

On the back of this page, make a scale drawing of the bulletin board. Each foot of the real bulletin board should be 1 inch (2.5 cm) on your diagram. Draw in the ribbon and balloons, too.

Music to Your Ears

Imagine that for your birthday, you receive a $25.00 gift certificate to the local music and video store. Using the ad below, select some things you would buy. Remember, the store will charge tax on your purchases. Don't go over $25.00!

Music and Video Express

Videos

$15.95 — 2 for $25.00

Compact discs   Cassettes   Cassette singles

$10.95 $8.95 $2.50

Blank cassettes — 99¢ each

ITEMS ORDERED

Items		Price	Quantity	Subtotal
1				
2				
3				
4				
5				
6				
7				
8				
9				
10				

Subtotal _____

5% Sales Tax _____

Total _____

71

                      © 1998 Good Apple GA1686

What Are the Chances?

You will be planning an activity with four other people. You need to decide if the group should go to a movie, ice-skating, or swimming at a local indoor pool. To be fair, make a spinner and write each person's choice in a section. Your group will then spin to see which activity is selected.

Directions

1. Write each choice in one section of the spinner.
2. Cut out the spinner.
3. Use a paper clip and a pencil to make the spinner work.

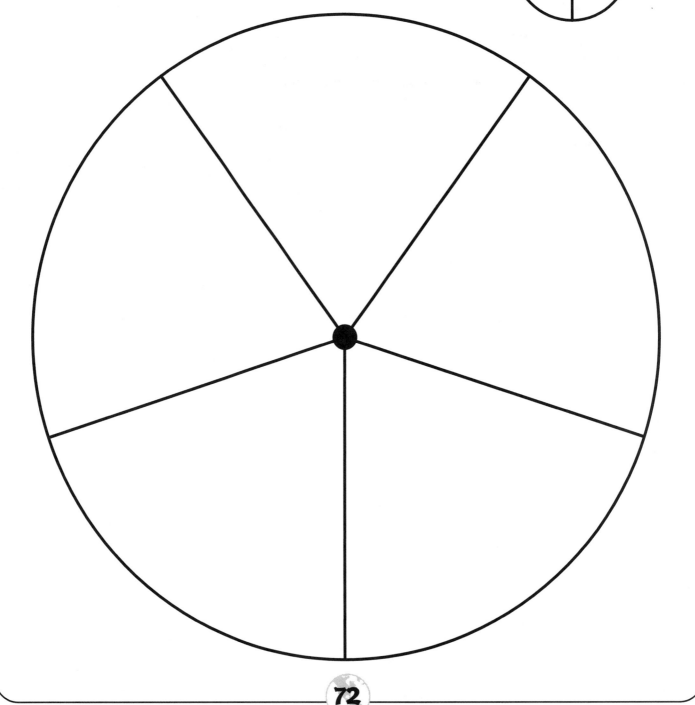

What Are the Chances?

Answer these probability questions about your spinner.

1. What is the probability that the spinner will land on:

   movie _____   ice-skating _____   swimming _____

   Explain your answer.

   _____

2. If you spin the spinner 30 times, how many times do you think it might land on:

   movie _____   ice-skating _____   swimming _____

   Explain your answer.

   _____

   _____

3. Which activity do you think the spinner will land on? _____

   Why do you think that? _____

   _____

4. Now test your predictions. Spin the spinner 30 times, and record the results in the chart below.

OUR GROUP'S SPINS

Activity	Tally	Totals
Movie		
Ice-skating		
Swimming		

5. Compare the results with the predictions. How close were your predictions to

   the results? _____

6. Do you think this spinner would be a fair way to select an activity for your group? Explain.

   _____

   _____

© 1998 Good Apple GA1686

Classroom Games

Imagine your class has been granted $100.00 to spend on classroom games. Work with a partner to come up with a plan for how to spend the money. Think about the number of students in your class. Try to purchase enough games so everyone can play something during parties or recess. Complete the table below to show what you plan to buy.

CLASSROOM GAMES TO ORDER

Game	Price	Quantity	Total	Money Remaining

Total Amount Spent: _____

On the back of this page, write a note to your classmates to convince them that your plan is best. Will everyone have a game to play? Have you stayed within your budget?

Games List

GAME	PRICE	NUMBER OF PLAYERS
Chinese Checkers	$7.99	2 to 6
Mastermind®	$6.79	2
Connect Four®	$11.49	2
Tri-Ominos®	$9.89	2 to 6
Outburst Junior®	$16.99	2 or more
Scrabble Sentence Cube®	$9.49	2 or more
Trouble®	$9.89	2 to 4
Battleship®	$12.99	2
Electronic Battleship®	$34.99	2
Monopoly®	$8.74	2 to 8
Sorry®	$13.99	2 to 4

© 1998 Good Apple GA1686

Real-World Literature Connections

Share some of these math-related books with your students. They will help you find more interesting ways to connect literature with real-world math!

Adler, David A. *Fraction Fun* (Holiday, 1996).

Anno, Mitsumaso. *Anno's Mysterious Multiplying Jar* (Putnam, 1983).

Aylesworth, Thomas G. *The Kids' World Almanac of Baseball* (Pharos, 1990).

Better Homes and Gardens, eds. *Better Homes and Gardens Step-by-Step Kids' Cookbook* (Meredith Books, 1984).

Branly, Franklyn. *Think Metric!* (Harper, 1973).

Burns, Marilyn. *The I Hate Mathematics! Book* (Little, Brown, 1975).

Carrie, Christopher. *Measurement* (Binney & Smith, 1987).

Clark, Steve. *Illustrated Basketball Dictionary for Young People* (Prentice-Hall, 1978).

Coerr, Eleanor. *Sadako and the Thousand Paper Cranes* (Dell, 1979).

Cushman, Jean. *Do You Wanna Bet? Your Chance to Find Out About Probability* (Houghton Mifflin, 1991).

D'Amico, Joan and Karen Eich-Drummond. *Math Chef: Over 60 Math Activities and Recipes for Kids* (Wiley & Sons, 1996).

Estes, Eleanor. *The Hundred Dresses* (Harcourt Brace, 1974).

Gibbons, Gail. *Marge's Diner* (HarperCollins, 1989).

Greenberg, Melanie Hope. *My Father's Luncheonette* (Dutton Children's Books, 1991).

Hollander, Zander, and Phyllis Hollander. *The Baseball Book* (Random House, 1991).

Hopping, Lorraine Jean and Christopher Egan. *Sports Math Mania!* (Sports Illustrated for Kids, 1996).

Kyte, Kathy S. *The Kids' Complete Guide to Money* (Knopf, 1984).

Sports Illustrated for Kids. Monthly magazine (Sports Illustrated).

Maestro, Betsy. *The Story of Money* (Clarion, 1993).

Markle, Susan. *Measuring Up! Experiments, Puzzles, and Games Exploring Measurement* (Simon & Schuster, 1995).

Moore, Carolyn E. *Young Chef's Nutrition Guide and Cookbook* (Barron's 1990).

Myller, Rolf. *How Big Is a Foot?* (Dell, 1991).

Schwartz, David M. *If You Made a Million* (Morrow, 1994).

Shannon, George. *Stories to Solve: Folktales from Around the World* (Morrow, 1991).

Stine, Jane and Jovial Bod Stine. *Everything You Need to Survive: Money Problems* (Random House, 1983).

VanCleave, Janice. *Janice VanCleave's Math for Every Kid: Easy Activities That Make Learning Math Fun* (Wiley, 1991).

Walker, Henry. *Illustrated Baseball Dictionary for Young People* (Prentice-Hall, 1979).

Williamson, Sara and Zachary. *Kids Cook! Fabulous Food for the Whole Family* (Williamson Publishing Co., 1992).

Wyler, Rose. *Math Fun with Money Puzzlers* (Silver Burdett Press, 1992).

Young, Woody. *Moneywise* (Joy, 1986).

Answer Key

Throughout this book, students have used data specific to themselves and their families. Therefore, many answers will vary. However, for each activity, make sure students have stayed on-task. Things to look for for each activity have been suggested, as well as specific answers for those activities in which data was provided.

REAL-WORLD CONNECTIONS

Newspaper Number Search, page 11

Answers will vary, but students should show an understanding of how numbers were used in the newspaper, leading them to conclude why numbers are important.

The Math Problem, page 12

Answers will vary. Make sure the problems represent math students do every day or fairly frequently.

Math All Around Us, page 13

Students' posters will vary, but should focus on the way math is applied to the theme.

Real-World Number Problems, page 14

1. $3 \times 9 = 27$
2. $100 \div 10 = 10$
3. $18 + 9 = 27$
4. $12 \div 3 = 4$
5. $6 + 60 = 66$

Problems will vary, but should demonstrate that students can correctly recognize everyday numbers.

How I Used Math Today, page 15

Answers will vary, but should reflect the real-world applications of math that students experienced during the school day.

DINING OUT

Food-and-Fun Family Restaurant, page 18

Yes, they're a bargain because the least expensive meal (hot dog or grilled cheese–$1.85), the least expensive drink (hot chocolate–80¢), and the least expensive ice-cream treat (99¢) add up to $3.64. A Kids' Meal Deal is $3.49, so it's less expensive than the cheapest combination of entree, drink, and dessert.

Video-Game Change, page 19

There are six possible combinations:

Dimes	=	Nickels	=	Total
5	50	0	0	50
4	40	2	10	50
3	30	4	20	50
2	20	6	30	50
1	10	8	40	50
0	0	10	50	50

Buying Bagels, page 21

1.–2. Answers will vary. Students should correctly add up their choices and figure out their change. The total bill should not exceed $5.00.

3. Some possible ways to buy 18 bagels include:
   1 dozen + 1/2 dozen:
   $4.99 + $2.99 = $7.98
   3 half dozens:
   $2.99 x 3 = $8.97
   individual bagels:
   50¢ x 18 = $9.00

Conclusion: 1 dozen + 1/2 dozen is the cheapest way to buy 18 bagels.

Bagel Possibilities, page 22

There are 12 possible combinations:

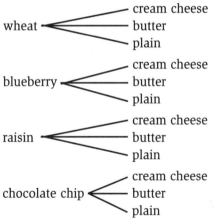

wheat — cream cheese, butter, plain
blueberry — cream cheese, butter, plain
raisin — cream cheese, butter, plain
chocolate chip — cream cheese, butter, plain

Bagel Glyph, page 23

Glyphs will vary, but should demonstrate that students understand the directions and can analyze the glyphs. Make sure students have also correctly tabulated the cost of the bagel breakfast according to the information on the glyph.

Home-Style Family Restaurant, page 24

Answers will vary, but students' prices should relate to the age of family members, and the total cost should be added correctly.

Burger Barn Design Contest, pages 25–26

Designs will vary. Make sure students have correctly colored the grids on page 26 according to the numbers on page 25, and that all items have been included.

Grand Opening Celebration, page 27

Times will vary, but performances should not overlap.

Burger Barn Problem Solving, page 28

1. 69¢ + 89¢ + 99¢ = $2.57
2. $2.09 + 89¢ = $2.98, $4.00 – $2.98 = $1.02
3. By adding Kate's desert (79¢) plus her change ($1.58), we get half the money she had left. So, Kate started with $4.74.
4. A cherry pie—it is the only dessert that costs 79¢.
5. She might have ordered a hamburger (59¢), French fries (89¢), and a soft drink (89¢); or a cheeseburger (69¢), French fries (89¢), and milk (79¢); or any food combination equaling $2.37.

How Many Should You Order?, page 29

Quantity	Food
20	French fries
5	hamburgers
10	chicken nuggets
15	cheeseburgers
12	colas
6	rootbeers
12	milk
10	chocolate sundaes (5 without nuts)
6	cherry pies
12	chocolate-chip cookies

IN THE KITCHEN

Sold by the Pound, page 32

Answers will vary, but students should show that they understand the concept of foods sold by the pound. Make sure students' costs are correct in relation to the price per pound.

Shopping List, page 34

2 lbs. green beans	=	$1.76
1 gallon milk	=	$2.69
1 box of cereal	=	$2.99
3 lbs. peanuts	=	$2.07
1 grapefruit	=	.50
Total	=	$10.01

Super Snack Mix, page 35

1. 5 batches—the mix serves 12 people.
   60 ÷ 12 = 5
2. Answers will vary. Students should base their answers on "1 dozen served."
3. Here are the amounts for 2, 3, and 4 batches of mix:

2 batches

Class of 13–24	16 pretzels
2 cups cereal	1 1/2 cups peanuts
1 cup marshmallows	1 1/3 cups chocolate chips
2/3 cup raisins	

3 batches

Class of 25–36	24 pretzels
3 cups cereal	2 1/4 cups peanuts
1 1/2 cups marshmallows	2 cups chocolate chips
1 cup raisins	

4 batches

Class of 37–48	32 pretzels
4 cups cereal	3 cups peanuts
2 cups marshmallows	2 2/3 cups chocolate chips
1 1/3 cups raisins	

Snack Riddles, page 36

1. 12 pretzels, 3 peanuts, 6 raisins
2. 9 pretzels, 5 peanuts, 10 raisins
3. 4 pretzels, 11 peanuts, 4 raisins
4. 4 pretzels, 4 peanuts, 8 raisins
5. 5 pretzels, 15 peanuts, 5 raisins

Create a Snack Mix, page 37

1. 4 raisins, 6 peanuts, 10 pretzels
   Ratios: 20% raisins, 30% peanuts, 50% pretzels
2. 4 raisins, 12 peanuts, 8 pretzels
   Ratios:
   raisins to peanuts: 4 to 12, or 1 to 3
   pretzels to raisins: 8 to 4, or 2 to 1
   peanuts to pretzels: 12 to 8, or 3 to 2

Rating Snacks, pages 38–39

Answers will vary, depending on the data students collect. Check to make sure students have accurately calculated the averages and ranked the snacks.

The Cookie Sheet, pages 40–41

Answers will vary, depending on the nutrition labels students use. Make sure students correctly plot the sugar and fat numbers on the graph on page 40, and that they correctly analyze this information on page 41.

Answer Key

SPORTS

Comparing Baseball Players, page 45

Answers will vary, but should reflect the stats students wrote on the chart for their players. Students should demonstrate that they understand the stats and recognize the higher, or better, numbers.

How Tall Are They?, page 46

Answers will vary. Make sure students correctly know how to convert feet to inches (or meters to centimeters), and that they can calculate the mean, median, mode, and range.

Through the Years, page 47

Answers will vary, depending on students' players. Make sure students accurately plot and analyze the players' batting averages on the graph.

Baseball Glyph, page 48

Students' glyphs will vary, but should accurately show information about the baseball player.

Batting Averages Bar Graph, page 49

Bar graphs will vary, but be sure they reflect the information presented by the class's glyphs from page 48.

Most Valuable Player, page 50

Answers will vary, but should reflect the players' stats. Players should be ranked correctly.

Ballpark Birthday, page 52

Step 1
1. July 13
2. 7 p.m.
3. beach towels

Step 2
1. $8.00 (1 adult and 1 child)
2. $10.00

Step 3
Answers will vary, but students should correctly add their foods and calculate the money remaining.

A Picnic at the Ballpark, page 53

1. 10
2. Answers will vary. Students should correctly match the age and price.
3. Answers will vary. Students should correctly add the admission prices.

Plotting the Hits, page 54

1. (1, 4)
2. (1, 19)
3. (7, 6)
4. (8, 2)
5. (16, 1)
6. (17, 17)
7. Answers will vary. A ball should be drawn in the general area of third base. The coordinates should match the ball's position.

Bowling Tournament, page 55

1. Estimates will vary.
2. 90
3. 95
4. 91
5. Melissa
6. Possible answer: To find an average, I added all Melissa's scores for a total of 285. 88 + 95 = 183. 285 − 183 = 102. So, I would have to bowl 102 to have the same average score as Melissa and tie for first place.

Scoring Baskets, page 56

There are 12 possible combinations:

# of 3-pt shots	# of 2-pt shots	# of 1-pt shots
3	0	0
2	1	1
2	0	3
1	3	0
1	2	2
1	1	4
1	0	6
0	4	1
0	3	3
0	2	5
0	1	7
0	0	9

Extension: 25%. Possible answer: I scored 9 of my team's 36 points. 9 is 1/4 of 36. 1/4 is the same as 25/100, or 25%.

Home or Away?, pages 57–58

Answers will vary, but should reflect the information on the chart on page 57. Make sure students understand how to calculate percentages.

79

Answer Key

TRAVEL AND ENTERTAINMENT

Weather Map Travels, page 61

Answers will vary. Check to make sure students understand how to calculate the mean, median, and range of the temperatures on the chart.

Weather Map Travels, page 62

Graphs will vary, but should accurately plot the high and low temperatures on page 61.

Weather Map Travels, page 63

Letters will vary, but should reflect the information on the weather chart on page 61, as well as additional information about the city students research.

Family Fun Parks, page 65

1. Answers will vary, depending on family members, but heights and admission prices should match.
2. Answers will vary.
3. Possible answer: It is a good idea for people 48 inches (120 cm) or over to buy a combo. If they buy separate tickets, it would cost them $52.00, but the combo ticket is $49.00. It would not be a good idea for a senior citizen ($31.00 for 2 separate tickets) or a child under 48 inches (120 cm) ($28.00 for 2 separate tickets) to buy a combo pass, because the separate prices are less than the cost of the combo ticket.

Aquarium Adventure, page 66

Answers will vary, depending on the family members, but the age and admission prices should match. Students should then figure out how many times they might visit the park, and multiply that number by the total family price to determine if the unlimited admission is a value.

Birthday Plans, page 67

For 11 children (10 guests and the birthday child) the cost is:
bowling — $49.50
miniature golf — $38.50
rollerblading — $52.25

Souvenir Bags, page 68

Answers will vary. Students should correctly total their choices and determine if they've stayed within the budget.

Refreshments, page 69

Answers will vary. Students should correctly total their choices and determine if they've stayed within the budget.

Party Decorations, page 70

1. 20 square feet (2 m²) of paper
2. 18 feet (5.5 meters) of ribbon
3. 6 yards (5.5 meters) of ribbon
4. 18 balloons

The scale drawing should be a rectangle that is 4 inches (10 cm) high and 5 inches (12.5 cm) long.

Music to Your Ears, page 71

Answers will vary. Students should correctly add the prices of the items, then correctly figure out the sales tax. Make sure they did not exceed $25.00.

What Are the Chances?, pages 72–73

Answers will vary, depending on the occurrences of each activity on the wheel. Students should recognize the probability in fractions of 1/5 or increments of 20%.

Classroom Games, pages 74–75

Answers will vary. Students should correctly subtract the game prices from the $100.00 starting figure, staying within the budget.